ISTANBUL

IN 3 DAYS 2024

A perfect exploring plan on how to enjoy top attraction places in Turkey for first timer visit with food guide, shopping, and many local secrets to save time and money

CLARA R. BURGHER

DISCLAIMER

The information contained in this book is for general guidance only. The author and publisher disclaim any liability for any loss, injury, or damage resulting from the use of this book. The information provided is not intended to be exhaustive or definitive, and travelers should always check with relevant authorities and sources for the most up-to-date information before embarking on any journey.

By reading this book, the reader acknowledges that they have read, understood, and agree to the terms of this disclaimer. The author and publisher make no warranties, express or implied, and disclaim any liability for any damages, including but not limited to indirect, special, incidental, or consequential damages, arising out of the use or inability to use this book."

TABLE OF CONTENTS

INTRODUCTION

Istanbul, one of the most fascinating cities in Europe or Asia, is known for its epic sunsets, faraway sounds of Namaaz, majestic minarets, and charming cats.
The word "East meets West" is overused, yet no other place fits the description so perfectly as Istanbul. The Bosphorus Strait divides Asia and Europe.
If I begin writing an introduction to this historically, culturally, and artistically rich city, I will be unable to stop typing.

BONUS

ISTANBUL
In 3 days 2024
TO GET YOUR
BONUS
TURN TO PAGE 58

ISTANBUL TRAVEL GUIDE

Quick history: Istanbul was previously the ancient Roman colony of Byzantium. In the early ages, it served as the imperial city of Constantinople. When the Ottoman Empire took the city in 1453, the Middle Ages of history began.

I won't go into detail on the history in the introduction, but I will cover it briefly in the itinerary for the majority of Istanbul's attractions. This can assist you have a better understanding of the location you're visiting.

Oh, and if you believe Istanbul is Turkey's capital city, you are mistaken. It is Ankara. Haha, you got it!

Istanbul, like many other famous cities such as Rome and Lisbon, was constructed on hills. Istanbul has a total of seven hills.

Many visitors to Turkey utilize Istanbul as a stopover before proceeding to Cappadocia, Pamukkale, or Ephesus. To really experience Istanbul, I suggest spending at least three days there.

Exploring Seven Hills in 72 hours is a daunting job, and those who adore the city will shake their heads in contempt. Still, this fantastic 3-day Istanbul itinerary has been meticulously planned to give you a taste of many various parts of the city.

Is it safe to visit Istanbul?

In all honesty, although parts of Istanbul's streets seem "dodgy," I felt largely secure, even at night. However, I must caution you of the different scams in the city, including pickpockets.
It's a large city, and you're often surrounded by hundreds of people. Pickpockets may easily steal your belongings without you knowing. However, this is not just a recommendation for Istanbul, but for many major cities, including Europe's most iconic cities.
Of course, I should mention that I did not go far from Istanbul's more touristic areas, which may have contributed to my feeling of security. Furthermore, there are many police officers on the streets, particularly on the city's major streets (perhaps as a result of the bomb incident at the end of 2022), making it even safer.

What is the ideal time of year to visit Istanbul?

Without question, summer is the most popular season for travelers to visit Istanbul. These are the months with the highest temperatures and

the longest days. However, these are the months in which costs are at their highest.
As a result, I suggest visiting the city during the off-season. Without a doubt, the finest months to visit Istanbul are March-May, as well as September and October. Of course, the weather will be cooler and there is a greater chance of rain during these months, but the reduced costs and fewer people will more than compensate.
For example, when I visited the city in early October, the temperatures remained nice, even though the days were no longer as hot. Regarding crowds, I believe that people are increasingly traveling during the shoulder season, and as a result, some of Istanbul's finest tourist destinations are still extremely crowded in October, for example.
If you want to get to know Istanbul in a more lively setting, you can always schedule a vacation around one of the city's major events. This may potentially be one of the greatest times to visit Istanbul.

Tulip Festival (April/May)
Istanbul Theatre Festival: October/November.
Akbank Jazz Festival (September/October)
Istanbul International Film Festival: April.

Finally, although it is possible (and nice) to visit Istanbul between December and February, you will likely experience chilly days and, maybe, snow.

What is the currency used in Turkey, and how do you pay?

The Turkish lira (TRY) is the national currency of Turkey. In April 2024, the currency rate against the Euro is 1€ = 34.60 TRY. Please keep in mind that this currency has seen historically high levels of inflation, therefore any prices referenced in the lira in this book may no longer be accurate. This is really the most probable outcome.

When it comes to payment, I was pleasantly surprised by how many establishments take credit cards (even in rural locales and for little amounts). Even so, you should always carry some cash since certain locations may not take credit cards.
I always paid with my Revolut card, which provides various benefits. One of the most significant benefits of using a Revolut card when traveling is that it does not impose fees for transactions in multiple currencies.

How can I get the internet in Turkey?

As soon as I landed in Turkey, I decided to get a SIM card at the airport. There were three possibilities, but I was advised to go for Turk Telecom, and the service was satisfactory.

- Vodafone 20 GB for 999 TRY
- Türk Telecom 30 GB – 999 TRY
- Turkcell 20 GB – 1199 TRY

Alternatively, you can purchase an e-SIM immediately before your vacation to save time when you arrive. For example, this e-SIM option offers a variety of options for various travel duration.

How To Get To Istanbul

Istanbul, Europe's biggest the city, is rather well connected. You can arrive at the city using different ways:

Plane: Flying is perhaps the most popular and maybe the most convenient option to get to the city. Istanbul has two major airports: Istanbul Ataturk Airport (IST) and Sabiha Gökçen International Airport. IST is the newest airport and the one closest to the city center, yet both are well-connected to many major cities throughout the world.

Bus: Istanbul is also well linked to other Turkish cities by bus, with several local bus companies providing routes to and from the city. I suggest utilizing Flixbus to acquire bus tickets; nevertheless, taking the bus to Istanbul might take a long time. Bus travel can be less expensive, however, Pegasus or Turkish Airlines provide relatively low rates between Turkish towns and other parts of Europe. So, I'd check into this before reserving a bus.

Boat: Istanbul is situated at the crossroads of Europe and Asia. As a result, whether you are traveling from the Bursa area or other locations along the Black and Aegean Sea coastlines, you can schedule a ferry to Istanbul.

Istanbul Itinerary Day 1 - The Historical Peninsula

If you arrive in Istanbul by plane, you might land at either Istanbul Airport (IST) or Sabiha Gökçen International Airport (SAW). In 2016, I arrived at Atatürk Airport, which is no longer in service. In November 2023, I traveled from the new Istanbul Airport (IST), and I was pleasantly impressed at how wonderful it is.

Istanbul has no lack of great hotels, and I like how you can experience luxury at a bit reduced rate. I appreciate Middle Eastern luxury standards since everything is more luxurious than average.

Tip: Avoid using taxis in Istanbul since the traffic is always bad. Get an Istanbul City Card and use it on metros, trams, buses, and ferries. Take advantage of Istanbul's fantastic public transportation system.

Book your Istanbul City Card at getyourguide.com

- **Ticket Name:** Istanbul: Public Transportation Card With Hotel Delivery

I had a lot of fun visiting Istanbul with this city card in my pocket since it made it so simple and exciting to go from one location to another.

I jumped on old red trams for fun and also used the metro.

1.)Start in Sultanahmet Square

Your first day will begin in Istanbul's Sultanahmet District, located on the European side of the city.

Walking around Sultanahmet Square is often one of the first things a traveler does while visiting Istanbul. The area features many popular tourist attractions that are all within walking distance of one another.

Furthermore, Sultanahmet Square, like any other "touristy" place, has a large number of cafés and restaurants, most of which I suggest you avoid.

Sultanahmet Square was formerly Constantinople's hippodrome and social hub. During that period, there was also horse racing in the region.

The most popular sights are Hagia Sophia and the Blue Mosque, but you should also see the Serpent Column, the Obelisk of Thutmose III (Obelisk of Theodosius), the Walled Obelisk, and the German Fountain. Most people who only have a day in Istanbul visit Sultanahmet Square.

2) Go to the Blue Mosque

often known as... Sultan Ahmet's Mosque

The Sultan Ahmet Mosque is breathtaking from the inside, and it is also free. This magnificent Turkish building is without a doubt one of Europe's most well-known landmarks. It is an imperial mosque, designed for members of the Ottoman imperial family.

The Sultan Ahmet Mosque is known as "the blue mosque" because its interior is covered with blue hand-painted tiles. They will be on the walls and ceiling.

The blue interiors look fantastic with the rich red carpet. The low-hanging lights and many windows provide incredible light, and the outcome is magnificent.

The Blue Mosque has six minarets, 5 major domes, and eight minor domes. It is hard to catch everything in one photograph, but you can walk to the center of the garden or courtyard with a wide-angle lens and capture the visible minarets and domes.

The building of this historical mosque was completed in 1616. The greatest light for shooting the Blue Mosque from the courtyard is around sunset. But, hey, I offer many more places for sunset photography in this book, so make your choice appropriately.
The mosque has a large courtyard, and when you enter, you will see worshipers doing noon

prayers. There is a separate portion inside for visitors and another for Islamic worshipers.
When you're inside, you must cover your legs, shoulders, and head, so please dress appropriately. I recall seeing a sarong rental facility at the entrance.
It is free to enter the Sultanahmet Mosque.

3) Visit Hagia Sophia Grand Mosque

Hagia Sophia is located right next to the Sultan Ahmed Mosque and will be free to visit beginning in 2023. Furthermore, it was

originally a Greek Orthodox Christian patriarchal basilica, then a mosque, then a museum, and now redeclared to a mosque again.
Because it was previously a costly destination to visit but is now free, there is often a long queue of people waiting outside the Hagia Sophia Grand Mosque.
If you like appreciating ancient architecture, you'll be interested to hear that Hagia Sofia is said to have influenced the history of architecture throughout history.

Hagia Sophia, built in 537 AD, features orange exterior walls. It was a significant landmark for Byzantine imperial ceremonies.
Hagia Sophia was an imperial Ottoman mosque from 1453 until 1931 before being converted into a museum in 1935. It was named after Sophia the Martyr.
The admission charge to Hagia Sophia was once 20 TL, however it is now free as of 2023.
If you want to bypass the lineups and purchase an admission ticket for Hagia Sophia in advance, I've highlighted the choices below for you.

- Hagia Sofia: Skip-the-Line Ticket includes Guided Tour: 30-Minute Tour @getyourguide

Ticket Name: Hagia Sophia Exterior Tour Optional ticket.

- The Hagia Sophia Fast-Track Admission with a Licensed Guide: one-hour tour at getyourguide

Ticket Name: Hagia Sophia with Old City Highlights Tour with the local expert.
There isn't much difference in what both tour guides provide, but it's always a good idea to check the most recent reviews before scheduling your tour or event.

4) Basilica Cistern

The Basilica Cistern is less than a 2-minute walk from the Hagia Sophia Grand Mosque. It is the biggest remaining Byzantine cistern beneath Istanbul city.

It appears in the famous James Bond film From Russia With Love. If you're a fan of Dan Brown, you've most likely read about this cistern in his book Inferno.

The Basilica Cistern entrance is located in Sultanahmet Square, between the Blue Mosque and Hagia Sophia. Inside the Basilica Cistern, there are 336 marble columns organized in 12 rows of 28 columns.

If you want to view the Basilica Cistern, I strongly recommend buying a skip-the-line admission ticket to avoid the inconvenience of standing and waiting. @getyourguide.com,
Ticket name: Istanbul Basilica Cistern Skip-the-line entry and an audio guide

Basilica Cistern has a fascinating history, which I will not go into detail about, but rather the most intriguing parts in my opinion. It was built in the sixth century but was closed when the Byzantine emperors relocated, after which it was utterly forgotten.
It was rediscovered in 1545, when a researcher was examining Byzantine antiquities in Istanbul and the locals informed him that they

could get water by lowering buckets in the dark space under their basements. The medusa heads and upside-down heads were very fascinating to me.
Basilica Cistern is unique and a fascinating location for taking unusual photographs.
The entrance charge to Basilica Cistern is 450 Turkish Liras per person.

5) Lunch at Pudding Shop

Pudding Shop is a historic restaurant/cafe in Sultanahmet Square that prospered in the 1970s due to its location on the hippie route. If you want to enjoy home-style traditional Turkish food you can choose and pick what you want on your plate and pay at the counter before eating.
I had salmon, kofte, mashed potatoes, salad, and caramel pudding. Overall, the lunch was fantastic, and the view from the window was very nice since it faced the bustling Sultanahmet Square.
My vegetarian pals sampled chickpeas, okra, aubergine, and barley. That dish was delicious to me as well. Of course, they also serve typical Turkish doner kebabs.

6) Visit Topkapi Palace (optional)

After lunch, go 500 meters to Topkapı Palace, which was formerly the primary residence and administrative center for the Ottoman Empire but is now a major museum.

This palace embodies the essence of true Turkish royalty. It is rather large and can take many hours to explore thoroughly.

It has a magnificent imperial gate, and four large courtyards on separate levels, each with its own set of sections within, a harem, an exterior garden, and several smaller courtyards. The Eunuchs also have their own courtyard in the harem.

Inside, you will be astounded by the Sultans' baths with golden grills, the imperial throne, the fruit chamber, and the many stained glass windows.

You will also be able to observe the panoramic view of the Marmara Sea from the palace. The garden area in the second courtyard features some pretty unusual trees, some of which are hollow on the inside due to fungus.
The entrance ticket for Topkapı Palace is 750 Turkish Lira per person.

> If you want to escape the queues and get an admission ticket to Topkapi Palace ahead of time, go to getyourguide.com and book this trip, which includes a guide.

Ticket Name: Istanbul: Topkapi Palace Guided Tour and Skip the Line

7) "Busforus" Sunset Tour

If you think this is touristic, please listen to me. Have you ever taken a hop-on-hop-off bus open tour? I did one a long time ago in New York City and discovered that it is the ideal way to view the sunset and all of Istanbul's wonderful attractions.

Book a Sightseeing Bus Tour at GetYourGuide.
Ticket Name: Istanbul: Two Continents Evening Bus Tour with Commentary

Considering Istanbul's chaotic traffic, using a taxi makes little sense. I definitely prefer local transportation, although you will miss the sunset.

I took a trip with Istanbul Tourism, and I was giggling when we got on the "Busforus" tour since it seemed so touristy. But as the bus journey began, I couldn't help but change my mind since I got a better perspective of all the attractions.

The trip began in the Sultanahmet district, then moved on to Eminonu, Karaköy, and Galataport, where I crossed the Galata Bridge and saw the Galata Tower in the distance.

We crossed the Bosphorus Bridge around sunset. I'll never forget the vista of the Bosphorus Strait at sunset from here. We also passed by Dolmabahçe Palace, and I was shocked at how beautiful it was.

Return to Your Hotel to Freshen Up.

After your Busforus city tour, take the metro back to your hotel and freshen up. Prepare to eat street cuisine in one of Istanbul's busiest neighborhoods.

8) Taksim Square and Istiklal Street for Street Food

If you took my advice and booked a suite at CVK Park Bosphorus, you'll just need to walk 5 minutes to the bustling Taksim Square. This is Istanbul's liveliest neighborhood, and I was surprised to see how busy it was even on a Tuesday night.

Stand in front of the Taksim Mosque and you'll find street food vendors, a classic red tram, and dozens of intriguing shops all around. Walk from here to Istiklal Street and eat your heart out.

The world-famous doner kebab is perhaps the most popular street food to sample in Istanbul, but I love kofte and vegan bulgur kebabs. Enjoy Ayran or sherbat with a sweet treat like Turkish delight, Tavukgöğsü (milk pudding), Halva, or Baklava.

Istanbul Itinerary: Day 2: Bazaars, Culture, and Food

If you thought your first day in Istanbul was enjoyable, you will be pleasantly surprised on your second day. Your Istanbul city card will also come in useful today, as we will be seeing several attractions that are more easily accessible by public transit than taxis.
Download an offline version of Istanbul's map from Google Maps to use when traveling by public transportation.

1) Spice Bazaar

Also known as Egyptian Bazaar or Misir Carsisi.

To reach to Spice Bazaar, take the yellow line metro from Taksim Tünel and get off at Eminönü. It is also referred to as Egyptian Bazaar and Misir Carsisi.
Enter the Egyptian Spice Bazaar through one of the high-arched doors to discover a magnificent inside bazaar with intriguing arched ceilings.

The spice market includes tea, nuts, dried fruits, and Turkish delights. It is smaller than the nearby Grand Bazaar, which is one of the next items on the list.

Even 30 to 45 minutes is enough of time to explore the charming Misir Carsisi and its intriguing shops.

2) Beta Yeni Han Café

Beta Yeni Han, a lovely café, is located toward the end of the spice market. You have plenty of time today to visit Istanbul's bazaars and cultural highlights, so stop here for a cup of Turkish coffee or tea.

While going through the small lanes of bazaars, the unexpected wide areas of Beta Yeni Han come as a pleasant surprise.

3) Grand Bazaar & Lunch

Walking 650 meters down the small passageways will lead you to another arched entry to a covered bazaar, Istanbul's Grand Market, which is huge.

The Grand Bazaar, one of the world's oldest and biggest covered marketplaces, entices with its labyrinthine alleyways and kaleidoscope of goods. It's a sensory voyage through vibrant textiles, beautiful ceramics, and the heady scent of spices. The Grand Bazaar is more than simply a bazaar; it's a cultural experience in which the past and present collide.

Istanbul's Grand Bazaar is iconic, and it should not be missed. It is a nice area to get away from the midday heat since it is covered.

Believe it or not, the Grand Bazaar is one of the world's oldest covered marketplaces, with approximately 4000 booths and 61 lanes. It also had 18 separate access points and was known as the "first shopping mall" in the world. Construction started as early as 1455/56.

The bazaar is so massive that it may overwhelm you! However, because of the interesting sights, people, and things, it could become one of the best places you visit in Istanbul. It is not only historically significant, but it also provides a delightful taste of Turkish culture.

The grand bazaar is located in Istanbul's Fatih neighborhood, between the Nuruosmaniye and Beyazit mosques. Walk around and visit as many streets as possible, and you can even have lunch here. After that, relax in the hammam.

4) Beyazıt Square

Beyazit Square, situated in the center of old Istanbul, is a thriving testament to the city's rich past and lively present. Nestled among a tapestry of historic structures and institutions, the square exudes an energy that reflects the old and contemporary.

The famous Beyazit Mosque, a 16th-century architectural marvel dominates Beyazit Square. Its unusual Ottoman style, with beautiful domes and thin minarets, lends majesty to the surroundings. The mosque's courtyard is a peaceful retreat, allowing people to rest and absorb the spiritual ambiance.

Because of its closeness to the Grand Bazaar, the area is alive with activity.
Beyazit Square also houses Istanbul University, a renowned institution established in the 15th century. The university's presence lends intellectual energy to the area, with students engaging in vibrant conversations or taking breaks in the neighboring parks.
As the day progresses, Beyazit Square changes. In the evening, the plaza comes to life with the sounds of everyday life. Locals and visitors converge in the nearby cafés and restaurants, creating a vibrant scene. The square, illuminated by the warm glow of streetlights, becomes a gathering spot where the city's heartbeat can be felt.
In essence, Beyazit Square exemplifies Istanbul's diverse identity. It expertly ties together the strands of history, spirituality, commerce, and academics to create a colorful tableau that embodies the essence of this dynamic city. Whether pulled by its architectural wonder, the appeal of the marketplaces, or the spirited energy of its people, Beyazit Square is a powerful invitation to experience Istanbul's multifaceted soul.

5) Suleymaniye Mosque

The largest mosque in Istanbul, the Süleymaniye Mosque, is located atop Istanbul's third hill. It is the biggest of Istanbul's imperial mosques, and many consider it the most magnificent. The mosque was rebuilt in 2010 at a cost of 21 million Turkish Liras.

From here, one can see Suleymaniye Mosque's vast courtyard as well as the Golden Horn and

Bosphorus Strait. There is also a hammam and a restaurant inside the mosque compound.

Return to Your Room to Freshen Up

6) Galata Tower for Sunset Panoramic View & Dinner

Walking over the Galata Bridge is a experience since it crosses the Golden Horn. It serves as a symbol of the connection between Istanbul's ancient and modern districts.

Locals fishing on both sides of the Galata Bridge is an intriguing sight to observe.

Cross the Galata Bridge, and you'll be able to view your next stop from a long distance. If you like perspectives, you'll appreciate this place since it provides the greatest view of Istanbul from above.

The Galata Tower is one of Istanbul's prominent monuments, standing proudly at 16.5 meters (54 feet). It is a stone tower that was built in 1348 AD.

The tower has nine floors and two elevators that take you to the seventh level, from which you must climb two floors on your own.

Please bear in mind that the waits outside Galata Tower at sunset are quite long, so plan accordingly. Even when there are large waits, they usually move quickly.

On top, there is an observation platform that provides a 360-degree view over Istanbul, the Bosphorus Sea, the Golden Horn, Topkapi Palace, the Blue Mosque, Hagia Sophia, and

many other sites. The observation deck is relatively small and resembles a ring around the tower.
The viewing platform on top of Galata Tower becomes jam-packed, so you may not be able to remain for long, but there are two restaurants on lower levels where you can eat and relax while admiring Istanbul's skyline.
There is also a flying stimulator, 3D Skyride, which costs an additional 25 Liras and lasts 10 minutes.
Galata Tower shuts at 8 p.m., however the restaurants may stay open later.
The entrance fee for Galata Tower is 650 Turkish Liras per person.

Nightlife in Istanbul’s - Galata District

After you've spent enough time at Galata Tower, take advantage of the active nightlife in this area. You can have dinner at one of the restaurants under the Galata Bridge before heading out to one of the clubs or bars.
Many bars in Beyoğlu provide outside dining and live music. Clubs can also be found here. Baraka in Beyoglu has live music on weekends. You can also go to Bizz Jazz Bar for Jass music,

Riddim for alternative, rock, or hip-hop music, and Mojo for pure rock.
When in doubt, you can always return to Istiklal Caddesi or Taksim Square, where you spent your first night in Istanbul on day one of the itinerary.

Istanbul Day 3 Itinerary

For your third and last day in Istanbul, I have two possibilities for you. You can choose a day excursion to the nearby islands or continue to explore Istanbul. If you don't want to spend the whole day on the Princess Islands, you can visit the attractions listed below to fall even more in love with Istanbul.

1) Food Tour (5-6 Hours)

Istanbul is a city rich in historical culture, and the best way to experience it is via food. I would not do a food tour in many places, but Istanbul is one of them.

One of the finest things I did in Istanbul was a cuisine tour, which I strongly suggest to you. There are numerous food tours available, and I believe it is preferable if these trips begin early so that you can relax and unwind in the evening.

Book a Food Tour at getyourguide.

Ticket Name: Istanbul: Guided Food Tour of Street Food and Markets.

We enjoyed a variety of kebabs, including meat on skewers, vegetarian kebabs made with bulger, pide, mussels packed with rice, Turkish delight, sherbets, and many other intriguing things. This was better than any five-star meal and well worth the cost.

I have selected a number of food tours, but I recommend this one since it begins at the right time and includes both the European and Asian parts of Istanbul.
Otherwise, you might check out this list of tours that I have compiled for you:

- **The Taste of Two Continents food tour:** A 6-hour food tour that begins at 9:30 a.m. and includes 9 stops. It goes to Istanbul's Asian side, namely the Kadikoy market. It begins at Hobyar Mahallesi.

- **Guided Tour of Street Food and Markets** This 6-hour tour begins in Rüstem Paşa, which is at one end of the Galata Bridge. You'll see both the Asian and European sides, as well as Kadikoy. You can start at 10:30 or 11 a.m.

- **Guided Food and Culture Tour:** A 5-hour evening food tour begins at 6 p.m. With a stop at Kardikoy, it covers both the Asian and European sides.

2) Turkish Hamam and Massage

A hammam is a typical Turkish bathhouse that generally includes a sauna, a scrub, and sometimes a massage. A few years ago, I read a humorous post about someone's first Hamam encounter, which piqued my interest in trying it myself. Of course, my experience was very different from hers.
There are several hammams in tourist locations, some of which cost up to 100 Euros. Keep in mind that each area has at least one ancient hamam, and the ones that locals frequent might cost as little as 100 liras. Some of the less expensive hammams may not seem to be clean, yet the heat and marble eliminate germs.

The Ottoman period is when traditional Turkish hamam, or bathhouse, originated. These were created for cultural, religious, and commercial reasons.

Cağaloğlu Hamam is Istanbul's most luxurious Turkish Hammam, attended by celebrities such as Cameron Diaz, John Travolta, Kate Moss, and Ophrah Winfrey. How did I know this? Because there is a hall of fame inside with photos.

Cemberlitas Hamami, located near the Grand Bazaar (Çemberlitaş Hamamı), offers a more upscale dining experience.
After the first thirty minutes of scrubs and massage, you may relax for a few hours in an attractive steam room and soak in the hamam. Like other hammams, there are separate areas for men and women, although the bathing practices are nearly same for both sexes.

Affordable and Traditional Hamams
If you're looking for something inexpensive and less touristic, consider Çemberlitaş Hamamı in Fatih. The admission fee is 25 Liras and the scrub is 10 Lira. Alternatively, try Gedik Ahmet Paşa Hamamı in Gedikpasa, Büyük Hamam in Kasımpaşa, or Aziziye Hamam on Istanbul's Asian side.

3) Sunset Cruise Over the Bosporus (Option 1)

Yes, the Bosporus Cruise is touristic, but it is a great opportunity to visit some of Istanbul's most intriguing sights that you would not be able to see in only three days. The mosques' high minarets are beautiful from a distance, and there will be plenty of picture possibilities.

There are several ticket sales points for the Bosporus cruise across Istanbul's tourist areas, however, not all of them are reliable. I took a pricey 2-hour cruise since I decided to go at the last minute while roaming around Sultanahmet Square.

Honestly, my pricey cruise was not unpleasant at all, and I truly liked it, despite the fact that I was alone. I didn't need to travel anyplace special; I was simply in Sultanahmet Square, and their office was just there.

Right before the trip, one of the staff members transported us all to the pier, which was only a 5-minute walk away.

If you'd want to look into better possibilities for your Bosphorus cruise than I did, check out the tours and tickets I've recommended for you below.

- Bosphorus Cruise from Eminonu Pier: This 90-minute cruise begins at the Eminonu Ferry Station (Turyol), which is located below the Galata Bridge.
  Ticket Name: Istanbul: Bosphorus Cruise with Audio App

- Dinner Cruise on the Bosphorus: a 3-hour cruise with unlimited drinks and food. Non-Turkish drinks will incur an additional fee.
  Ticket name: Istanbul Dinner Cruise on the Bosphorus

- Sunset Bosphorus Cruise on a yacht: A 2.5-hour cruise on a beautiful yacht that includes a free local drink.
  Ticket name: Istanbul: Bosphorus Sunset Cruise on a Luxurious Yacht.

- Bosphorus Dinner Cruise with Entertainment is a 3-hour tour aboard a luxury yacht that includes views, food, beverages, and entertainers.
  Ticket Name: Istanbul: Bosphorus Dinner Cruise & Show with Private Table.

- Hop-On/Hop-Off Bosphorus Cruise: You may disembark at four different locations and rejoin the boat after 60 or 120 minutes.

All of the tours listed above are unique in their own way. I didn't have many alternatives while in Istanbul, but I would have chosen a smaller boat or a yacht since mine was a bit too packed.

Fortunately, I was bringing my own water since the water on the boat was quite costly.
When purchasing your ticket, bear in mind that it is pointless to pay more for a special seat. People will stand in front of you, blocking your view, regardless of where you sit.
Spend two hours in the evening on a sunset cruise around the Bosphorus straits. Opt for the tiny wooden boats so that the guide can better explain the facts as you travel to the Bosphorus Bridge and back to Asia.
Sehir Hatlari, a state-run company, offers a 2-hour cruise for just 120 Turkish Liras, departing at Eski Kadıköy Pier. They also offer a 3-hour option, but I think that's a bit much. Two hours is more than plenty. Check their website before visiting since they occasionally only provide sunset cruises on Saturdays.

4) Dinner at Oligark

One of the most fanciest and delicious meals I had in Istanbul was at Oligark, a waterfront restaurant that overlooks the Bosphorus Strait. It is a really elegant restaurant and bar, however, the pricing in Euros is actually rather reasonable.

The views, service, and food at Oligark are absolutely outstanding, and the experience should not be missed. I got the most wonderful (chee kofta) Çiğ köfte, lavash (lavaş), beef on skewers, and lentils, many other things that tasted heavenly.

Option 2: Çamlıca Hil for Sunset and Dinner

If you don't want to take the Bosphorus cruise at sunset, I have another alternative for you. Camilca Hill is Istanbul's highest point, located on the Asian side. From here, you can see the Golden Horn and the Bosphorus, as well as the panoramic view of Istanbul.

Camilca Hills are divided into two sections: Little Camilca Hill and Big Camilca Hill. This point refers to Big Camilca Hill in Üsküdar.

To access Çamlıca Hill from Taksim or Sultanahmet Square, take a tram to Eminonu Docks. From here, take a boat to Uskudar and then the 9U bus to Camlica Hill. Of course, you can take a taxi for the whole route or part of it.

You can enjoy the panoramic view while simultaneously visiting one of the cafés or restaurants. They are less pricey than those at Sultanahmet.

After spending the previous two sunsets in comparably busy (but magnificent) spots - Galata Tower and the "Busforus" Bus Tour - the sunset experience at Camilca Hill will be a welcome change. Many people claim that this is the finest sunset in Istanbul, but I'll let you decide.

Princes' Islands Day Trip (Option 3)

Many people refer to them wrongly as Princess Islands or Princess Islands, although they are really "Princes' Islands" and are a group of nine islands on Istanbul's Asian side. They are called after the exiled princes and monks who were put here during Byzantine and early Ottoman times.

Don't expect to relax on a beach on these "resort-esque" islands. Instead, these islands provide a cultural or historical experience. You'll get the impression that time stopped here some decades ago and never moved forward.

One of the most intriguing aspects of visiting the Princes' Islands is the ban on motorized vehicles. As a result, these islands provide a welcome respite from Istanbul's bustling life and traffic sounds. Instead, you'll witness horse carts and Victorian houses.

To get here, use a fast ferry provided by IDO or search for Istanbul Liners. These ferries leave from Kabatas or Eminönü, near the Galata Bridge. You can order ferry tickets to and from the Princess Islands here. Alternatively, you can arrange for a trip that will pick you up from your Istanbul hotel (if it is conveniently situated) and transport you to and from the Princess Islands, including lunch and sightseeing. Büyükada is the most popular island, with others being Kınalıada, Burgaz, and Heybeliada.

Tip: *Make sure to check the schedule so you don't miss the last ferry out of the islands.*

Accommodation in Istanbul

I've been to Istanbul twice, first in the Sultanahmet area and again around Taksim Square. I was pleased with both venues but concluded the second was a better option. To book a hotel, visit booking.com.

Here are some of my suggestions for various budgets:

- CVK Park Bosphorus (Room with a Sunrise View). CVK Park Bosphorus is conveniently positioned near the bustling Taksim Square, therefore this hotel wins in terms of location. The buffet breakfast served included both traditional Turkish breakfast items but also international essentials

- Amiral Palace
- Byzantium Hotel & Suites
- Pera Palace
- Angel's home
- Cheers is the most popular hostel chain in Cheers, with locations all around the city.

Some popular spots to consider staying in are:

- **Sultanahmet** is Istanbul's historic core, home to several of the city's most renowned attractions, such as the Hagia Sophia, Blue Mosque, and Topkapi Palace.

- **Taksim** is Istanbul's modern, cultural, and economic center, and it's an excellent pick for anyone looking for shopping, dining, and nightlife options.

- **Beyoğlu** is a popular area for staying in Istanbul. It is famous for its cultural and historical sites, as well as its trendy cafés and nightlife.

- **Galata:** This neighborhood, known for the Galata Tower, exudes chic and hip vibes. It is located across the river from the Old Town and is known for its hilly streets and old structures.

Where to go after Istanbul?

Istanbul to Cappadocia

Cappadocia features an otherworldly environment filled with strange formations, fairy chimneys, and hundreds of hot air balloons in the sky.

Istanbul to Pamukkale

Pamukkale's magnificent limestone thermal pools have made it a popular spa destination since antiquity. You will undoubtedly fall in love with this place, which is mostly blue and white.

Three Days in Istanbul Itinerary: Final Thoughts

This itinerary takes into account Istanbul's culture, sights, and uniqueness. It is a tried-and-true plan based on my two journeys to Istanbul. Don't strive to see everything since Istanbul can be hectic. Remember to be spontaneous and enjoy yourself.

TRAVEL JOURNAL

Date:

Location:

Budget:

DAY 1

Personal Itinerary

TODAY'S LOG

6 AM	
7 AM	
8 AM	
9 AM	
10 AM	
11 AM	
12 PM	
1 PM	
2 PM	
3 PM	
4 PM	
5 PM	
6 PM	

PLACES TO GO

REMINDER

Date:	
Location:	
Budget:	

DAY 2

Personal Itinerary

TODAY'S LOG

6 AM	
7 AM	
8 AM	
9 AM	
10 AM	
11 AM	
12 PM	
1 PM	
2 PM	
3 PM	
4 PM	
5 PM	
6 PM	

PLACES TO GO

REMINDER

Date:

Location:

Budget:

DAY 3

Personal Itinerary

TODAY'S LOG

6 AM	
7 AM	
8 AM	
9 AM	
10 AM	
11 AM	
12 PM	
1 PM	
2 PM	
3 PM	
4 PM	
5 PM	
6 PM	

PLACES TO GO

REMINDER

My Adventure Experience